United in Christ

Preparing for Christian Marriage

Scott Stiegemeyer

Concordia Publishing House • Saint Louis

3558 S. Jefferson Ave., St. Louis, MO 63118-3968
1-800-325-3040 • cph.org

Manufactured in the United States of America

6 7 8 9 10 11 12 13 14 32 31 30 29 28 27 26 25 24

CONTENTS

✤✤✤✤✤

Engaged to Be Married

Congratulations! God loves marriage. He will bless you.

You have heard the frightening statistics regarding the percentage of couples who eventually divorce. Maybe you grew up in a home affected by divorce. Good marriages do not just happen. They require much work and sacrifice. There are many forces, spiritually and socially, that battle against the union of marriage.

Consider the earnest warning the pastor gives at the beginning of the rite of Holy Matrimony:

> Marriage is not to be entered into inadvisedly or lightly, but reverently, deliberately, and in accordance with the purposes for which it was instituted by God.

This is why you must carefully prepare for this lifelong commitment. The fact that you are reading this book is a good sign. It shows that you are intent on learning all that you can to help ensure a happy, Christ-filled life together. Reading relationship books, attending retreats, and meeting with your pastor are all excellent ways to strengthen your relationship and provide a healthy start to your married life.

The goal of this book is twofold: First, to examine what God's Word teaches about marriage, relationships, and family. What does Scripture say about your relationship, your marriage, as well as issues that could cause you challenges down the road? Second, this book will help you engage in identifying the strengths and weaknesses of your relationship.

While this is certainly a book about your love for each other, in another sense, and perhaps more important, this is a book about the Lord Jesus Christ, the Bridegroom, and His love for His resplendent Bride, the Church. It is by the design of the Creator that marriage, as an institution, proclaims the higher mysterious beauties of God's mercy and love.

What Is Holy Matrimony?

Marriage is a socially and legally recognized contractual union of one man and one woman. Every society has marriage in some form, though it is becoming more scarce in certain areas, such as northern Europe. Although various cultures may have defined it differently, marriage is not ours to update or abolish. God instituted marriage in the Garden of Eden before the fall into sin (Genesis 2:18–25) as a means to preserve and prosper human life in His good creation.

The great reformer and pastor, Martin Luther, writes:

> This is the true definition: Marriage is the divinely instituted and lawful union of a man and a woman in the hope of offspring, or at least for the sake of avoiding fornication and sin, to the glory of God. Its ultimate purpose is to obey God and to be a remedy for sin; to call upon God; to desire, love, and bring up children to the glory of God; to live with one's wife in the fear of the Lord; and to bear one's cross.

Our Lord Jesus said that God Himself joins the man and woman together in marriage (Matthew 19:6). So marriage is holy because God, who is holy, instituted it; He makes the two individuals into one flesh, and He blesses all creation through this union. Because God instituted marriage, it is used in Scripture as an illustration of the relationship between God and His people. This reality is particularly recognized in the Church's teaching concerning holy matrimony.

> "Therefore a man shall leave his father and mother and hold fast to his wife, and the two shall become one flesh." This mystery is profound, and I am saying that it refers to Christ and the church. (Ephesians 5:31–32)

Are We in Love?

There is much confusion about the nature of love. It is frequently mistaken for a mere emotion, a feeling in the gut or the heart, a state that one can fall into and out of almost randomly. Certainly, love brings all sorts of pleasant feelings. Popular media refer often to love, suggesting that it is all you need for a relationship to succeed and that if you are in love, nothing else matters. But what does it really mean to be in love? Is love an emotion? Or is it something more?

The English language is imprecise in this matter. We use a single word to say: "I *love* ice cream." "I *love* my country." "I *love* my children." On the one hand, we are referring to things we enjoy very much, such as ice cream. But your love for your country is such that you might lay down your life in its defense. How many people would die for ice cream? Clearly, though we are using the same verb in every sentence, we mean vastly different things.

The New Testament uses two Greek words for "love." *Phileo* refers to warm affection, such as friendship. It refers to the feelings of fondness one person has for someone or something. One might say this is emotional love. The second word for love, *agape*, is not based on feelings or emotion. *Agape* is a favorable regard based on one's choice, a commitment. It is often allied with notions of sacrifice, one for the other.

One of the most familiar Bible verses is: "For God so loved the world, that He gave His only Son . . . " (John 3:16). It is important to note that this verse does not say, "For God so loved the world that He felt warm emotions." His gift of His Son was a result or consequence of His commitment, His deep resolve to secure our salvation. God's love does not remain hidden in His heart. Rather, it results in action, specifically the action of self-giving or self-sacrifice.

St. Paul connects Christ's self-sacrifice and human marriage in Ephesians 5. He understands that husbands and wives are a model or representation of the relationship between God and Israel, between Christ and the Church. Thus Paul instructs men: "Husbands, love your wives, as Christ loved the church and gave Himself up for her" (Ephesians 5:25). Jesus' life was not taken from Him; rather, in His commitment to our salvation, He willingly gave up His life. Christ's offering of Himself upon the cross for us is the model for a man to follow in his love for his wife. We know from the events in the Garden of Gethsemane (Luke 22:39–46) that Jesus did not have fond feelings about being tortured and dying. He experienced fear and deep anguish. But no pain would deter Him from laying down His life to save us, in full accord with His Father's will for Him.

This is the definition of real love. God is love. It is God's nature to give. And He gives Himself to us fully. Real love considers the needs and well-being of the other person first, regardless of cost. The love between a man and a woman in marriage seeks to be that *agape* love, that voluntary determination to serve the other person. Over the years, emotions will wax and wane, but love, *agape*, chooses to serve the other because of thanksgiving and gratefulness for the mercy shown to the sinner in Christ. With this understanding, hear how Paul talks of the loving relationship:

> [*Agape*] is patient and kind; [*agape*] does not envy or boast; it is not arrogant or rude. It does not insist on its own way; it is not irritable or resentful; it does not rejoice at wrongdoing, but rejoices with the truth. [*Agape*] bears all things, believes all things, hopes all things, endures all things. (1 Corinthians 13:4–7)

Is Marriage a Sacrament?

Whether we call something a sacrament or not is irrelevant. But it is important to observe those things that God has given, according to His institution, and to rejoice in their respective blessings. Traditionally, Lutherans define a sacrament as rites commanded by God and to which the promise of grace has been added (Apology of the Augsburg Confession, Article XIII). The essential part of a sacrament is a clear promise or word from God. Combined with something earthly, such as water or bread and wine, it becomes, as St. Augustine stated, a visible word from God (*Tractates on the Gospel of John*, 80:3). By this strict definition, marriage would not be a sacrament. Although God works blessings through marriage, an act He instituted, it is not a Means of Grace, that is, it does not impart the forgiveness of sins. Marriage is unlike a sacrament because it is not given to every person who believes, and nowhere does Scripture say that marriage grants the forgiveness of sins. As our Confessions point out, marriage is unlike Holy Baptism, which provides forgiveness of sins through the washing of baptismal water, or the Lord's Supper, through which God imparts forgiveness, life, and union with Him.

What about a Civil Ceremony?

Marriage is a matter of the secular realm. All people may marry, whether Christian or not. And God surely blesses these unions, because He sends the rain on the just and the unjust alike (Matthew 5:45). Nevertheless, church weddings are to be encouraged for Christian couples.

> Because marriage is a gift of the Creator that is not negated by the fall into sin, it may be performed by civil authorities, apart from the Church. While such civil ceremonies are good according to "civil righteousness," they do not speak the Lord's blessing or implore His grace and aid for a sanctified marriage and home. (*LSB Agenda*, p. 61)

Although a church wedding is not absolutely necessary, it is a magnificent way to begin your married life. You gather in God's house with the congregation and God's called minister to pray for God's blessing upon your marriage and to sanctify your union with the promises of God's Word.

A wedding performed in a courthouse by a judge is no less valid than a church wedding in either the eyes of the state or the eyes of God. As a temporal arrangement, marriage is a matter of the state, so being married in the church by a clergyman is not necessary for the marriage to be valid. But the blessings of a church wedding are abundant. The church's rite of Holy Matrimony "supplies what the government cannot give—the Lord's Word, the prayer of the Church, and the Lord's dependable promise of help and protection . . . and offers prayers that [the couple] may live in godly harmony" (*LSB Agenda*, p. 62).

Under Assault

God loves marriage. He is exceedingly pleased when one man and one woman pledge their love and faithfulness to each other.

However, there is one who does not love marriage. He does not rejoice with you. He is not pleased when a man and a woman declare their love and faithfulness to each other before the world. This one is our archenemy, Satan. He is a fallen angel who, with his followers, both terrestrial and otherwise, wages war against God. Naturally, Satan and his angels are powerless against God directly, so he exerts his energies against those made in God's image and likeness.

> Then God said, "Let Us make man in Our image, after Our likeness. . . ." So God created man in His own image, in the image of God He created him; male and female He created them. (Genesis 1:26–27)

A happy marriage repulses the devil. Thus he will do anything he can to undermine marriage as an institution, including attacking your marriage. Be alert to his ways. He will capitalize on your weak points both as individuals and as a couple. This is why it is important to inspect yourselves in the mirror of God's Word. You must discover and acknowledge your weaknesses. Expose them. Receive private Absolution where necessary, and gird yourselves for battle, for there is indeed a war taking place, one for the sanctity of your marriage and the health and happiness of your family (Ephesians 6:10–13).

What about Divorce?

Before discussing marriage and wedding plans, agree with each other that divorce will never become a consideration. Agree that it is not an option for you, that you will stick together through thick and thin, no matter what. If you cannot say this honestly, then how can you honestly speak your vows at your wedding?

Are there no exceptions? In the New Testament, Jesus speaks to the permissibility of divorce on the grounds of sexual immorality:

> It was also said, "Whoever divorces his wife, let him give her a certificate of divorce." But I say to you that everyone who divorces his wife, except on the ground of sexual immorality, makes her commit adultery, and whoever marries a divorced woman commits adultery. (Matthew 5:31–32)
>
> And Pharisees came up to Him and tested Him by asking, "Is it lawful to divorce one's wife for any cause?" He answered, "Have you not read that He who created them from the beginning made them male and female, and said, 'Therefore a man shall leave his father and his mother and hold fast to his wife, and the two shall become one flesh'? So they are no longer two but one flesh. What therefore God has joined together, let not man separate." They said to Him, "Why then did Moses command one to give a certificate of divorce and to send her away?" He said to them, "Because of your hardness of heart Moses allowed you to divorce your wives, but from the beginning it was not so. And I say to you: whoever divorces his wife, except for sexual immorality, and marries another, commits adultery." (Matthew 19:3–9)

Divorce is clearly our action to separate what God has joined together. Scripture speaks plainly that God hates divorce (Malachi 2:16). Unlike contemporary society, God considers marriage to be a lifelong commitment.

Even in cases of infidelity, repentance and reconciliation is the better course. But when that does not appear to be possible because of our hardness of heart, because of our inability to forgive as we have been forgiven (the Lord's Prayer), divorce is tolerated as an unhappy outcome.

ARE WE READY TO BE MARRIED?

RELATIONSHIP PITFALLS

UNREALISTIC EXPECTATIONS

The romantic sentimentalism found in much of popular culture—novels, movies, and television—has given many people a skewed understanding of what to expect from love and marriage. Although no-fault divorce has been common for several decades, and millions of adults are children of divorced parents, people still have a dreamy, overly sweetened belief about finding their soul mate, "the one," of having a storybook wedding and living happily ever after. People fall in love and believe that getting married will make them happy and possibly solve their problems.

Marriage is a beautiful institution, but it is not a magic cure-all. If your relationship is built on an unstable foundation, getting married will only make those problems worse, not better. While some people are blinded by an overly rosy idea of love and marriage, those who have watched the marriages of others crumble can develop an aversion to marriage. Neither extreme is healthy.

One common, but unrealistic, expectation is that the personality traits, attitudes, or behaviors of one's partner will somehow change in a significant way by virtue of being married. You are in serious trouble if your relationship is founded, even unconsciously, on the expectation that one or the other of you will become a different person. This does not mean that people cannot or do not change—they can and do. All the time. In fact, you can count on the fact that over time both of you will change in some ways—and perhaps not in ways either of you might choose.

All of us have things about ourselves that we ought to try to change: bad habits, personality flaws, mistaken beliefs. Our heavenly Father is re-creating us even now by the power of His Spirit through His Word. This is what the Bible calls sanctification, a process that will be perfected only in heaven. *Sanctus* is the Latin word for "holy." God makes us holy, as He is holy, not by beating us over the head with rules and regulations, but through the transformative power of the Gospel. People can and do change with the help of God. But the majority of people, the majority of the time, reject the idea that they need to change. The problem, they insist, is with someone else.

If there are traits in the other person that annoy you now, count on these traits being present for the rest of your lives together. Can you live with that? As awkward and as painful as this might be, it is better to discover and discuss these issues now, before the wedding, than to need to deal with them years later. Does your betrothed have a quick temper? Is he or she a heavy drinker? These are red flags you should not ignore.

I am not saying that a person must be perfect before you can get married. No one but God alone is perfect. The intent is not to discourage you, but to help you face your future realistically. It may be a generalization, but the best predictor for future behavior is past behavior.

If you have religious differences, are you expecting to convert your beloved once you are married? Be honest with yourselves. Of course, God works conversion in the hearts of people all the time. But this is not something upon which we should base our future happiness in marriage. It is a mystery too deep to fathom why some people hear the Gospel in its fullness and believe while others hear it and do not believe. If you and your future spouse are on different pages when it comes to religious faith, it is wise to expect that this will always be the case. You can pray for God to bring you both into unity in the truth, but God has not promised to convert everyone. We should not found our lives upon promises that God has not made. There is no question that there have been many happy marriages in which husbands and wives hold to different professions of faith. Can you be happy together without this being resolved in advance? How will you raise your children when it comes to matters of life, death, ultimate meaning, the existence of God, or views of right and wrong?

WORKAHOLISM OR OVERCOMMITMENT

We want it all: kids, prosperous careers, a second house at the lake, nice cars, nice clothes, exotic vacations, and a comfortable retirement. Even in our most economically depressed times, the majority of Americans wallow in wealth compared to two-thirds of the world's population. We have become accustomed to a certain way of living, with gadgets and accessories and comforts we identify with a life that is "good."

In order to reach our material goals, it is common for both spouses to work, to put in overtime, to take on more and more. This is not a criticism of the many hardworking people who live paycheck to paycheck and struggle, at times, to make ends meet. But when the long hours and hectic schedules are in the name of career advancement or material acquisition, you must consider the costs in other areas of your life.

Relationships require time. You must spend time together or you will grow apart. And if one or both of you are mentally and physically exhausted during your time off, then the relationship will not receive the care and attention it needs to remain healthy.

You demonstrate your values by how you invest your time. Make sure your marriage and family rank high on the list, higher than your personal ambitions, no matter how wholesome and all-American they might be. What are some practical ways that you can maintain your relationship as a high priority? Many couples schedule a weekly date night even after the wedding. Make the necessary arrangements. Call the babysitter. This ensures that you will focus on each other. Another idea is to commit to eating dinner every night at the dining room table with the television off. Communicate every single day. As a Christian couple, pray together. Read Scripture and devotional literature together. Keeping God in your marriage will further cement the bond of love you share.

Addiction

Addiction is sinful, without question. That is not to say that in God's eyes addicts are worse sinners than anyone else. Jesus said that everyone who sins is a slave to sin (John 8:34). Morally, no one can claim superiority. In fact, if you find yourself feeling superior to someone else, you have committed the damning sin of pride.

Although addicts are not inherently inferior in the eyes of God, their particular failings make healthy relationships extremely challenging. Addicts in recovery understand that they are slaves. Their lord and master is their drug or addictive activity. When their addiction has the upper hand, they will do things to hurt you in order to achieve their fix. It will be as though you do not exist or matter. Addicts need love and the mercy of Jesus Christ, as we all do. But unless the addict has proven a desire to recover by seriously and consistently taking steps toward wellness, life with this person may be unpleasant, hurtful, and perhaps even harmful.

The psychology and biology of addiction is daily better understood, and there exist many excellent paths for treatment. If addiction is something that you wrestle with now, be honest and get help. For the sake of the people you love, have the courage to do something positive. If addiction runs in your family, know your weaknesses, acknowledge your limitations, and do not allow the devil to get that foothold in your life.

Selfishness

Selfishness is the opposite of love. Ask yourself if you are a giver or a taker. Do you think only of yourself? Selfishness is, in a sense, the most fundamental sin, the bedrock of all sinfulness. Selfishness motivated Eve to disregard the warnings of God and heed the serpent's call. Selfishness is pride. It is placing yourself in the center. And nothing is more deadly to a marriage.

Philippians 2:3 makes clear that love always means that you put the other person before yourself: "Do nothing from rivalry or conceit, but in humility count others more significant than yourselves." But be careful. The pendulum could swing too far in the opposite direction. Scripture does not say that you are supposed to ignore completely your own needs or wants. It is better to express your needs rather than suppress them. While it might seem obvious to you what you need in a relationship, and you may wish that your beloved understood intuitively how to express love to you, this is frequently not the case. Love does not require you to disregard completely your own emotional, mental, and physical needs. The trouble comes when an individual exalts his own needs above those of the people around him. This is not easy, and you will spend the rest of your life practicing at not being selfish. That is because it is native to our fallen condition to be radically self-centered.

There is no love greater than the love that God shows toward His rebellious children by granting the forgiveness of their sins. This is one reason why it is extremely important for your family to be present regularly in God's house, where the Good News of free salvation is purely preached and the Sacraments are administered according to Christ's institution. As you hear that you are the recipient of unselfish divine love, that God in Christ has made the ultimate sacrifice on your behalf, God's Spirit melts the hardened me-centered heart.

INFIDELITY

Luther's explanation of the Sixth Commandment states:

> You shall not commit adultery.
>
> *What does this mean?* We should fear and love God so that we lead a sexually pure and decent life in what we say and do, and husband and wife love and honor each other.

Even in sexually open societies, infidelity is usually seen as a bad thing. No matter how open-minded and accepting people claim to be, the pain of knowing that your beloved has been romantically or sexually unfaithful is severe. Betrayal is one of the most profound injuries we can inflict on others because it is inherently something that can occur only between those who love each other. Strangers do not betray; friends betray, lovers betray.

Sexual betrayal is more than physical sexual activity involving a third party. Both men and women experience powerful temptations to stray. Typically, for men, this begins visually. Jesus said in the Sermon on the Mount: "You have heard that it was said, 'You shall not commit adultery.' But I say to you that everyone who looks at a woman with lustful intent has already committed adultery with her in his heart" (Matthew 5:27–28). Infidelity has already begun when a man or a woman sexually desires someone other than his or her spouse. Men, let your desire be for your wives. Women, let your desire be for your husbands. Remind yourself that you have no right to possess the body of another—either in actuality or in your imagination.

Temptations, however, are inevitable. It is impossible to exist in contemporary society, which is flush with provocative images, without succumbing to illicit carnal desire. Martin Luther once compared temptations to birds. We cannot prevent the birds from flying over our heads, but we do not have to let them build nests in our hair.[1] In other words, we must diligently train ourselves not to dwell on those suggestive images or thoughts that inevitably enter our mind. For it is in dwelling on them that the cravings of the body, tainted with sin, are stirred. Sexually immoral thoughts are like weeds encroaching on the flower bed. If you keep them at bay, they can, to a great extent, be managed. Pluck them out immediately. But if you indulge yourself a little bit, failing to keep watch, what began as a small encroachment can quickly overtake the bed, choking out the flowers.

Infidelity is a problem of the heart, not merely the body. Jesus said, "For out of the heart come evil thoughts, murder, adultery, sexual immorality, theft, false witness, slander. These are what defile a person" (Matthew 15:19–20a). Sexual immorality defiles a person. And it defiles a marriage.

One biblical author writes: "Let marriage be held in honor among all, and let the marriage bed be undefiled, for God will judge the sexually immoral and adulterous" (Hebrews 13:4). And St. Paul issues this severe warning: "But sexual immorality and all impurity or covetousness must not even be named

---

1 *Through Faith Alone: 365 Devotional Readings from Martin Luther* (St. Louis: Concordia, 1999), reading for March 8.

among you, as is proper among saints. Let there be no filthiness nor foolish talk nor crude joking, which are out of place, but instead let there be thanksgiving" (Ephesians 5:3–4).

Chastity begins in the mind and the heart. Our culture is saturated with sexually charged images and innuendos. The battle for a clear head and clean heart is a daily one. We can begin to gain control over wayward thoughts by directing our minds away from the titillations of the world and toward those things that are pure and spiritually edifying. St. Paul writes: "Finally, brothers, whatever is true, whatever is honorable, whatever is just, whatever is pure, whatever is lovely, whatever is commendable, if there is any excellence, if there is anything worthy of praise, think about these things" (Philippians 4:8). Do not permit tempting images and thoughts to take hold of you. Paul further states: "Take every thought captive to obey Christ" (2 Corinthians 10:5b). Although we fail often in our struggle against the devil, the world, and our sinful flesh, God is merciful to all who repent and turn from their sin. Daily—morning, noon, and night—the Christian humbly bends the knee, imploring God to be gracious, to provide deliverance from the power of sin, to provide strength against temptation, and to pardon failings. God is trustworthy, and He promises to forgive. From this promise, we draw strength to resist temptation and are given the Holy Spirit, who gives us new and pure hearts.

5 C's to a Successful Marriage

Compatibility, Commitment, Communication,
Conflict Resolution, Confession

Compatibility

Birds of a feather flock together, but opposites attract. Two people of widely different personalities and viewpoints might get along famously because they complement each other. The excitement of difference can fuel curiosity and discovery in a relationship. However, without areas of meaningful commonality, common interests, shared values and beliefs, realizing a lasting relationship will be fraught with difficulty.

You do not have to agree on everything, but you do have to respect and appreciate the differences. A lot of this has to do with personal temperament. How tolerant are you of difference? Are your differences irritations or endearments?

For example,

one of you is rabidly punctual and the other is constantly late;

one of you is almost obsessively tidy and the other is a slob;

one of you enjoys frequent outings with friends and the other is a homebody.

These differences do not have to be a negative. Instead, focus on identifying the things in your relationship that you both enjoy. What interests or goals do you share? How can you support each other when your interests and goals vary? Accept that you will not always want the exact same things. That is all right as long as you also explore those areas you share in common. Attend lectures or concerts, work on hobbies, volunteer at church, go skiing. Give each other room to be individuals, but look for places of overlap and make the most of them. Make sure you know each other well before getting married. This process of exploration and discovery takes time.

Commitment

Fear of commitment is a common reason people do not marry. What is there to be afraid of: the loss of freedom? restraint of one's individuality or identity?

Commitment is not based on a feeling. How you feel about each other on a given day in the future may go up or go down. But you can weather the storms of feelings in the confident assurance of your mate's pledge of faithfulness. Commitment is an act of the will. It is a discipline. And marital commitment is for life, or else it should not be made at all.

Every healthy marriage must be built on trust. The marital pledge of love and faithfulness is a promise. You can trust each other because of these promises you have made and kept. Read often the promises you intend to make on your wedding day—these marital commitments you will make to each other are for life. If you cannot say that, then these promises should not be made at all. After your marriage, continue to look at these promises often, read them again as you watch the wedding video on your anniversary, recall them together as you witness the weddings of friends and family members as a reminder of the basis for your relationship.

Is it scary? It can be. But know that God will bless your fidelity with a peaceful, happy home. Making a commitment does, in a sense, restrict personal freedom. However, instead of worrying about what you are giving up for the other person, focus on the stability and comfort of knowing that your beloved is yours without qualification, and that nothing and no one can interfere in what you share. As you grow together and as your relationship matures, it will become easier to pay less attention to what you do not have and more attention to what you do have together.

Use your engagement as a time to strengthen your commitment, love, and trust. Determine together strategies that you will use to make this relationship a healthy marriage. Do not let divorce even be a consideration. With that firm and stubborn resolve, and a tender loving attitude, you will go the distance.

Communication

Men and women are different, especially when it comes to communication. In part, this is because men and women often have different emotional needs. Understanding these differences is key to establishing healthy communication.

One difference is experienced in how we handle stress. This is a generalization, but typically men are fixers. They like to attack the problem and make it better. They are doers. Women are more likely to need to talk things out first. Talking about the situation and their feelings is a critical part of how they deal with stress, whereas men often do not excel at talking about their feelings.

So when a woman has a bad day at work or an aggravating afternoon with the children, she might need a caring ear to listen and a supportive shoulder to lean on. The man wants to get right to the action part. He is frustrated when clear solutions do not present themselves right away. Although women also want to accomplish things, they need to process it verbally. When they do not get that opportunity, they may feel unloved.

In communicating with their wives, husbands need to learn the art of listening without always wanting to hit the fast-forward button to get to the action. Provide a sympathetic ear. Show your wife you love her by helping her process her stress in an unhurried conversation with a trusted partner. Wives, understand that your husband is not impatient with you. His way of loving you is by rescuing you. That is his instinct, and it is why he wants to jump into solution mode right away. Husbands, ask questions to find out more about how your wife is feeling about things. Be genuinely interested.

Emotionally, women need to be assured that they are loved. This needs to be expressed to them in meaningful ways. Little things such as cards and flowers tend to mean a lot more to women than men, because these tokens communicate emotions.

For a woman, the well-being of the household is often the pressing daily concern. Men are more quickly satisfied that things are good enough: the roof is still attached to the house, there is a reasonable amount of food in the refrigerator, therefore, all is well. But women are more likely to think of all the other necessary details of life. And thank goodness they do. Do the kids have shoes that fit? Does the family have a good dentist? Will the new living room upholstery go with the paint on the walls? It is not that men are unconcerned with such matters; it is just that these things are frequently more important for a woman's sense of well-being. Men need to understand that. These are not accidents. It is how our ever-loving Creator intends a man and a woman to complement and complete each other.

There once was a television advertisement about choosing the right broker. It emphasized the importance of clear communication. The ad began with a man lying on a couch, talking about a dream, presumably to his psychiatrist. When the patient looked to his doctor for a response, the man taking notes in the chair beside him began to speak in a foreign language. The patient just stared, bewildered, and the voiceover made some remarks about the importance of having a financial advisor you can understand.

This television ad can illustrate the importance of communicating in marriage. Unlike doctors who use too much technical jargon or brokers who assume their clients understand more about finance than they do, couples do not have to overcome literal limitations of vocabulary. But people do speak different languages, as it were, when it comes to expressing love.

Best-selling author Gary Chapman explains that there are basically five different "languages" that people use to express love within a relationship. Everyone speaks all five languages to some extent, but according to Chapman, everyone has one primary love language.

In summary, the five languages are: Quality Time, Words of Affirmation, Gift-giving, Acts of Service, and Physical Touch. You and your partner each speak one of these five languages as your primary means of communicating your love for the other person. Your primary love language shapes not only how you speak, but it also shapes how you hear. In other words, if you express your love primarily by gift-giving, that is also how you perceive love being communicated back to you.

- **Quality Time** refers to spending time together enjoying each other's company. For some people, this can mean an evening on the couch watching television or, for others, a special evening out.
- **Words of Affirmation.** There are people who express their love primarily by heaping praise and words of support onto their beloved. "I love you." "You are so beautiful." "I really appreciate all that you are doing." And so forth.
- **Gift-giving** refers to giving gifts, spontaneously, large or small. The man who brings flowers to his bride just because. The wife who places little candies in her husband's lunch bag.
- **Acts of Service.** This refers to all those things that people do for each other that are not necessarily a lot of fun but need to be done. Mowing the grass. Making the beds. Shopping for groceries. Patching the roof. Of course, every family does these things. Husbands and wives do these things for each other all the time. How is this anything special? While every household has chores, some people are eager to do them for their loved ones. And they especially enjoy it when someone does something similar for them.

- **Physical Touch.** This does not have to mean sexual touch; simply hugging, holding hands, or giving the occasional unsolicited foot rub can fulfill a person's need for physical touch.

It is quite likely that you and your beloved do not share the same primary love language. In a strong relationship you will learn to be bilingual, that is, you will learn to recognize and honor each other's primary language.

Conflict Resolution

God loves peace. Jesus is the Prince of Peace. It pleases the Lord when we keep peace and work for peace. Jesus said, "Blessed are the peacemakers, for they shall be called sons of God" (Matthew 5:9).

However, into every human relationship there comes conflict. It is inevitable because we are all internally corrupted by sin. In fact, one definition of original sin comes from the Latin *curvatus in se*, which means being curved in upon yourself. Because our nature has been polluted, we all have a tendency to put ourselves first, to think only of what we desire or need.

People are givers or takers. There is a little bit of both in each of us, but usually you will be much more of one than the other. Very often, one person in a marriage is a giver and the other a taker. This can, for a time, have the appearance of harmony. There might not be a lot of visible conflict, but underneath a storm may be brewing. If the discrepancy is serious enough, the giver will become emotionally and physically exhausted. The taker will not be satisfied either, because takers never are. You could give a taker all you have and it will not be enough. Most likely, this situation will erupt into irritations, insults, and brokenheartedness.

It should be obvious that two takers will not be able to stay together long. The ideal is for both of you to be generous givers in the relationship. Give freely. Give daily. Give sacrificially. That is Christlike. Put the needs and interests of your mate before your own, and do so willingly. If both husband and wife are consistently devoted to serving the other person, everyone's needs get met and happiness will result. Being a giver in a relationship means that you cannot always "do your own thing." You may have to do the other person's thing sometimes, which might not always be fun or pleasant for you. All relationships require sacrifice, and all sacrifices hurt.

There is a healthy way to make peace and an unhealthy way. The unhealthy way is when a person is so averse to conflict, so allergic to raised voices or strong emotions, that he or she seeks to placate the upset individual, almost at any expense, simply to maintain a quiet status quo.

The key is to find the balance. Being quarrelsome is wrong, but constantly caving to the demands of one dominant person in the name of peace is not good either. It can lead to one spouse being bullied by the other, which is not how love works. Submissiveness is essential to a marriage, but it has to work, at times, in both directions. The traditional view of male headship in the home does not license the man to bossily lord himself over his wife. Rather, in love, he will respect and cherish her wants and feelings more than his own. And she will do likewise toward him.

Conflict can come about through a variety of ways. Some people are difficult to get along with because they are overtly aggressive. Aggression is when one person pushes his or her agenda onto others without taking into consideration what they think or how they feel. For example, "I am going to go play cards with the boys even though I promised to spend the evening with you." Aggression is when someone is inconsiderate, selfish, bossy, or openly hostile.

Other people are passive-aggressive. Passive-aggressive behavior is a defense mechanism when one person gives the appearance of going along while resentment seethes beneath the surface. The passive-aggressive person feels constantly exploited or unappreciated. His or her underlying bitterness often boils over into other areas of life. An example of this would be when a person agrees to fulfill a responsibility but then either "forgets," chronically procrastinates, or sulks. Pent-up frustration may be released at seemingly random times, unrelated to the true sources of the tension.

Both of these are unhealthy ways of coping with anger and are unbecoming to the Christian way of life. Neither of them are helpful behavior patterns in a marriage. Very likely, you are unaware of the times when you are exhibiting aggressive or especially passive-aggressive behavior. Learn more about these responses so that you can recognize them in yourself and find better ways of coping.

Now I am going to say something that may surprise you. Conflict is not always entirely bad. Addressing a clash of interests openly and honestly may be uncomfortable but frequently will result in a healthier relationship. Avoiding conflict at all costs can sometimes severely harm the health of a relationship. One should do all one can to lessen the opportunity for conflict. And by conflict, I do not mean fighting. Not all conflict is fighting. Not all arguing is fighting. Learn the rules of conflict in marriage so that when you disagree or when you must argue, it does not become a fight.

Conflict Dos and Don'ts

- **Don't assume the other person magically knows how you are feeling.**
- **Don't think that you always know the other person's motives.**
- **Don't assume the other person can read your mind.**
- **Don't assume that you can read the other person's mind.**
- **Don't dredge up the past.**
- **Don't resort to name-calling.**
- **Don't assume the worst. Be careful about jumping to conclusions. You might not like where you land.**

- **Do be respectful.**
- **Do speak as you would like to be spoken to.**
- **Do try to put the best construction on things.**
- **Do forgive, just as God forgives you.**
- **Do consider the point of view of the other person.**
- **Do ask God to help you resolve your conflict.**
- **Do listen carefully. You have two ears, but only one mouth. Maybe that is God's way of telling you to listen twice as much as you talk.**

It is not necessary for you always to agree on every single thing. As husband and wife, you will be "one flesh," but that does not erase your distinctive personalities. You do not have to like all the same foods, enjoy all the same pastimes, or share exactly identical opinions on every topic. A little variety adds spice to life. Learn how to appreciate or enjoy the uniqueness of your mate. Part of the endless delight of marriage is the ongoing discovery of your lover's specialness as you grow closer to the other person. One sure way to create resentment is to insist that your mate conform to your image in every way.

Between two human beings, disagreements will arise. These might be large and significant. Or they might be small and relatively insignificant. Wisdom knows how to tell the difference. If an irritation can be overlooked, it should be. Character is learning not to magnify minor irritations into major squabbles. However, when it comes to irritation, there can be a cumulative effect. Wearing a badly fitted shoe for an hour might give me a sore toe. But wearing it all day, with that constant rubbing, will give me a blister. Taming those features of your personality or behavior that you know irritate others is part of what it means to be a grown-up.

It is important to add that not all conflicts in a relationship are necessarily about matters of right and wrong. Often conflict can be over differences of opinion, taste, or preference. When my wife and I are sitting in the same room, it is probable that one of us is uncomfortable with the temperature. I tend to feel like it is too warm; she tends to feel it is too cold. How we deal with this situation can be an example of compromise. I could constantly put the air conditioner on full blast in the summer and open the windows in the winter. She could, on the other hand, put the thermostat on high in the winter and turn off the fans in the summer. The best thing for both of us is to learn the art of compromise. We each have to make the comfort of the other person our highest priority. Maybe I can tolerate the room a degree or two warmer, and she can wear a thicker sweater.

CONFESSION AND FORGIVENESS

"Love means never having to say you're sorry." We have heard this declaration repeatedly, but it is wrong. Perhaps the intention is to say something like: "I love you so much, I will always forgive and accept you, so you don't even need to apologize." The forgiver may not need an apology, but the forgivee needs to apologize.

Another common saying is that love is blind. Early in a relationship, everything might be rosy and bright. You are both still putting your best feet forward. You put each other on pedestals, or you worship the ground your beloved walks on. But let us be honest: no one is perfect. Understanding yourselves as sinners is not only crucial in your relationship before God, it is also essential for the success of your marriage.

By acknowledging your sinfulness, you are open to hearing God's word of pardon. A heart calloused and hardened against sin is not able to love or be loved. Know how to say you are sorry. Be honest enough to admit when you are at fault. As you become more aware of your own personal failings and of God's amazing grace, you can become more patient and able to forgive others.

A word must be included about repentance. We talk highly of the power of forgiveness in a relationship, and rightly so. But forgiveness without repentance is an express ticket to nowhere. The word for repentance in the Hebrew language of the Old Testament means "to turn." In the Greek language of the New Testament, the word means "to change one's mind." Repentance, then, is when a person turns from his wrong attitude or behavior. It involves a change of mind.

If this turning and changing of mind does not occur, then there may need to be temporal sanctions of some kind to bring about that desired change of heart. They say that the definition of insanity is to continue doing the same thing while expecting different results. When you are sinned against, you must let go of your anger and resentment toward the offending party or risk poisoning yourself. However, that does not mean that there might not need to be consequences imposed so the offender can learn to think differently and turn, that is, repent.

Have no doubt, Christ Jesus died for the sins of all people. It is extremely liberating when a person realizes this. In fact, it releases the shackles of death and hell itself. This is the Gospel: Christ Jesus died for sinners. The Bible does not say, "Behold the Lamb of God who takes away the sin of the world, except for *me*." It says, "Behold, the Lamb of God, who takes away the sin of the world!" (John 1:29). Period! Pure and simple. The blood of Jesus covers a multitude of sins.

God's grace and mercy are free, but they are not cheap. In other words, salvation came at a precious price, the death of God's one eternal Son. To receive the benefit of God's forgiveness, already purchased in full, repentance is necessary. It is not optional. One does not simply receive absolution and then willfully keep on sinning. It is impossible to love God while also loving your own sins. You must love the one and hate the other. The two are not compatible. To embrace your sin is to actively reject God and vice versa. Of course, in the complexity of human life, we do both many times daily.

The Christian life is a struggle for as long as we live in this world. The forces of spirit and sinful flesh are perpetually at war inside us. In Christian theology, we call this *simul Justus et peccator.* It means that believers are simultaneously sinners and saints. We are reckoned by God to be saints by virtue of Christ and His sacrifice on our behalf. Yet we continue to transgress the Law of God in thought, word, and deed. It is a paradox.

If you put two people together long enough, they will inevitably sin against each other. That is the state of our condition until the resurrection on the Last Day when our glorification in Christ will be made perfect. Meanwhile, we must find ways to live together in peace. Repentance and forgiveness are the empowering dynamic of our life together in this world. The wrongdoer admits his guilt and determines to change his behavior. And the other party graciously grants pardon. The Golden Rule is "do unto others as you would have them do unto you." This applies here as well. Forgive as readily as you would like to be forgiven. This is the key to a happy marriage. When both husband and wife abide in this dynamic, their marriage will be able to weather any storm.

What Is Wrong with Premarital Sex?

Premarital sex is much more accepted by society today than in past generations. The world asks, "As long as you love each other and the consent is mutual, what is wrong with sex outside of marriage?" Perhaps that is how you feel about the subject, even if it is not something you would prefer to discuss with your pastor.

God's law is unambiguous. The Sixth Commandment is: "You shall not commit adultery" (Exodus 20:14). As discussed above, Martin Luther's explanation states: "We should fear and love God so that we lead a sexually pure and decent life in what we say and do, and husband and wife love and honor each other." Sex, with all its joys and responsibilities, belongs to marriage, and by this commandment, God wants to protect marriage.

Christians object to premarital sex not because they have a low opinion of sex—quite the contrary. It is the world that coarsens it by implying that sex is purely recreation. Christians honor sex much more highly than the world by abstaining from it until the proper time and limiting it to only one partner.

Having sex is a matter of trust and commitment. You make yourself physically and emotionally vulnerable by stripping naked and engaging in the most intimate physical acts of affection. In the physical union, there is also an emotional bond. Scripture says that the two shall become one flesh, meaning that, in the bodily union, there is a deeply personal bond. Therefore, such intimacy is not something that should be rushed or taken casually. The body is not just a plaything that can be toyed with for discrete moments of pleasure and then put away until the next playtime. You and your body are one. When you put your body into situations of vulnerability, your heart is there also, even though it is possible to develop calluses on the affections.

When God places restrictions on our freedoms, it is not because He is arbitrarily trying to oppress us or keep us from having fun. The laws of God are given for our benefit. One of the functions of God's Law is to act as a curb upon our actions. Why do we have curbs along the roads? They keep traffic from slamming into the pedestrians. Only by driving within the boundaries of the curbs will you safely reach your destination. God limits our sexual lives not to make us unhappy, but rather to ensure our happiness. It might seem like a good idea to take a shortcut and drive over the curb and across the lawn, but the likelihood of destruction and injury is too great. It is so much better to restrain our desire for unbridled liberty and stay within the lines. God's will is always best.

Is It Okay to Live Together before the Wedding?

What is wrong with living together? On the one hand, it is not technically the living-in-the-same-house part that is wrong; it is premarital sex that God forbids. Hypothetically, a couple could insist that they share a domicile for economic reasons, for convenience, or for other reasons but that they do not sleep together. In such cases, the couple should understand two things. First, they are certainly going to give everyone the impression that they are sexually intimate because that is typically the case for couples who live together, thus giving the appearance of sinning. Second, even if they are making a sincere attempt to lead chaste lives, being in such constant proximity will subject them both to extraordinary temptation. It is a bad example for a Christian couple to set and does not honor God's name. It is unwise, no matter how you approach it. Following are some of the myths about cohabitation.

We Can See If We Are Compatible

You would not buy a car without first taking it for a test drive, right? However, love does not view the other person as a commodity. You do not have to live together in order to find out if you are compatible. There are many ways to get to know each other besides cohabitation. One way would be to enjoy a long engagement. It is a good rule of thumb to make sure you have known a person through all four seasons before entering the contract of marriage. Do not be hoodwinked by the romantic proclivities of our times with its fantasy of love at first sight. Spend ample time getting to know each other.

This Will Help Divorce-proof Our Marriage

Without question, cohabitation has become much more common in the past several decades. Once, the majority considered such behavior taboo. Now it is far more accepted. Although living together has become more common, the divorce rate has not declined; rather, the divorce rate has risen. This is not to say that the one directly causes the other, but the idea that living together will make you less likely to divorce later is unsubstantiated.

Society Has Accepted It

Societal acceptance is not the basis for determining right and wrong. For Christians, God's Word is the foundation for our beliefs and values, including our views of sexuality. Rather than accepting the lifestyle, Scripture commands: "Flee from sexual immorality. Every other sin a person commits is outside the body, but the sexually immoral person sins against his own body" (1 Corinthians 6:18).

The Pastor Is Just Being Judgmental

It is not the pastor who condemns sex outside of marriage; rather, it is God, who is the author of marriage. It is not the role of the pastor to be your bedroom cop. He has no desire to be seen as some kind of morality enforcement officer.

"We're not supposed to judge," someone will say. The Bible does warn us not to judge others or we will be judged. But that has become one of the most misquoted, misapplied passages in the whole New Testament. Jesus wants us to avoid any sense of self-righteousness. Do not bother taking the speck out of your brother's eye while you have a plank in your own (cf. Matthew 7:3). Jesus hates hypocrisy. He requires His followers to consider their own hearts and lives under the light of God's Law. And He requires us to be humble and not to consider ourselves superior to our neighbors.

However, Jesus does not mean that His followers must be moral relativists. It does not mean that everything is okay—that what is right for you is right for you and so forth. Not at all. God's Word has many clear commands regarding human behavior. The believer understands that he must faithfully observe the commandments of Scripture while at the same time avoiding a self-righteous attitude.

When a Christian pastor instructs people in the positions of Holy Scripture, he is being faithful to his calling. He must, even when it is inconvenient to do so, proclaim and explain the will of God. He should do so in humility and with compassion and tact. But a pastor cannot give tacit approval to actions and attitudes that God finds offensive.

If your pastor, or any Christian, points out your sin to you, you should say, "Thank you." Those who call your attention to your sins have most likely done you a good turn. If we remain in our sins, stubbornly defending behaviors that are condemned by God, we are in serious danger of eternal wrath. In such cases, the loving thing for your pastor to do would be to warn you gently and direct you to repentance and forgiveness.

So what are the options when your pastor or another Christian approaches you about cohabitation? This will not be easy. You must remember that your pastor is the called servant of God in that place to teach, serve, and—occasionally—correct the flock. Here are two possibilities: move out until the wedding or have a civil ceremony right away with a religious service of blessing to follow at a later time.

WHAT ABOUT "MIXED" MARRIAGES?

As a rule, it is considered a poor pastoral practice to perform weddings when neither the groom nor the bride is a member of the congregation. The pastor has a divine call to shepherd the flock to which he has been called, not serve as the local representative of the state for hire. But there will be occasions when a member of the congregation will become engaged with a non-Lutheran and desire to have a church wedding.

MARRYING A CHRISTIAN OF A DIFFERENT CHRISTIAN DENOMINATION

A Christian should always choose a faithful believer as a mate, but it is no sin for a Lutheran to marry a non-Lutheran Christian. There are many happy marriages between Christians of different professions of faith. However, differences in religious confession should not be brushed off as minor details. The unfortunate disagreements throughout history that have resulted in the multitude of denominations and religious organizations are often quite important. If you are unfamiliar with the particular teachings of your church body and why they matter, then for the sake of your own spiritual well-being, it would be good to take instruction with your pastor. Only then will you be able to intelligently discuss what you really believe from the Word of God and why you believe it. The goal of this premarital process is for you and your betrothed to arrive at a greater unity of heart, mind, and spirit, and having a better understanding of your faith is part of that process. In addition to premarital counseling, perhaps a review course in basic doctrine for the two of you would be worthwhile.

Marrying a Non-Christian

" 'All things are lawful,' but not all things are helpful. 'All things are lawful,' but not all things build up" (1 Corinthians 10:23). Your religious beliefs are an integral part of your identity. If your spouse-to-be worships a different god or professes no religious belief at all, then there will always be a significant part of you that he or she will never fully understand.

If your intended is not opposed to you freely practicing your faith, a civil wedding could perhaps occur, but a Christian wedding would not be appropriate. One pastoral theology text describes it this way: "The Christian marriage service is written as though it involves *Christians*. It includes pastoral *blessings*. These are not light matters."[2] Since the Christian wedding service includes trinitarian references and addresses the one true and only God, it would be hypocritical for a nonbelieving person to stand before a congregation and make vows before a deity he or she does not acknowledge. Consult with your pastor about ways in which he and your congregation can be supportive while not violating your beloved's integrity or conscience.

2 Norbert H. Mueller and George Krause, *Pastoral Theology* (St. Louis: Concordia, 1990), 208.

HOLY MATRIMONY: UNITED IN CHRIST

THE ORDER OF SERVICE

The rite of Holy Matrimony provides a context of praise, Scripture, and prayer within which "the Church through her pastors gives the heavenly Father's blessing to the willing consent and solemn promises of a man and woman. In this way, the Lord's blessing elevates the legal marriage to holy matrimony, where His Word and promise are clearly proclaimed. Martin Luther acknowledges this purpose of holy matrimony when he wrote in his *Marriage Booklet* that 'when someone asks us [the pastor] to bless them in front of the church or in the church, whether to pray over them or even to marry them, we are obligated to do so. . . . For whoever desires a prayer or blessing from the pastor or bishop, indicates thereby (even if he doesn't actually say so with his mouth) what kind of peril and necessity is approaching and how great is his need for divine blessing and common prayer for the estate into which he is about to enter. For one daily encounters all too often the kind of misfortune the devil serves up in the estate of marriage through adultery, unfaithfulness, discord, and all kinds of misery.' Therefore, the Lord speaks His blessing to those who are married so that they may faithfully keep their vows" (*LSB Agenda*, p. 61).

THE INVOCATION

P In the name of the Father and of the ☩ Son and of the Holy Spirit.
C **Amen.** *Matthew 28:19b*

The invocation of the name of the triune God and the sign of the cross recalls for us our own Baptism. In Holy Baptism we were immersed into the death and resurrection of Jesus, and it is at our Baptism that we were first called children of God. Here at the onset of our worship it is clear that this is a Christian ceremony and that those to be united are baptized into Jesus Christ and confess their faith in Him. Not simply an opening salute, these words are both a prayer that calls upon the triune God to graciously oversee the service and a confession of the Christian faith.

ADDRESS TO THE CONGREGATION

P Dearly beloved, we are gathered here in the sight of God and before His Church to witness the union of this man and this woman in holy matrimony. This is an honorable estate instituted and blessed by God in Paradise, before humanity's fall into sin.

In marriage we see a picture of the communion between Christ and His bride, the Church. Our Lord blessed and honored marriage with His presence and first miracle at Cana in Galilee. This estate is also commended to us by the apostle Paul as good and honorable. Therefore, marriage is not to be entered into inadvisedly or lightly, but reverently, deliberately, and in accordance with the purposes for which it was instituted by God.

In God's plan, the couple coming before His altar is to be a living example of the communion that all people individually and collectively may share in God through Christ Jesus. The pastor's address to the congregation at the beginning of the service of Holy Matrimony, therefore, explains for all who are assembled the purposes of marriage. This statement of the purpose of marriage, and the willing and deliberate desire of the couple to live in mutual love, is what forms the basis of the promise to be spoken later in the service.

The union of husband and wife in heart, body, and mind is intended by God for the mutual companionship, help, and support that each person ought to receive from the other, both in prosperity and adversity. Marriage was also ordained so that man and woman may find delight in one another. Therefore, all persons who marry shall take a spouse in holiness and honor, not in the passion of lust, for God has not called us to impurity but in holiness. God also established marriage for the procreation of children who are to be brought up in the fear and instruction of the Lord so that they may offer Him their praise.

For these reasons God has established the holy estate that *name* and *name* wish to enter. They desire our prayers as they begin their marriage in the Lord's name and with His blessing.

These opening words in the rite outline three divine purposes and functions of marriage: companionship, delight, and procreation. There could be added a fourth, proclamation of the Gospel.

I. Companionship and Community

> " . . . intended by God for the mutual companionship, help, and support that each person ought to receive from the other, both in prosperity and adversity."

In the beginning, when God created the heavens and the earth, He concluded each day by noting that it was good. On the sixth day, He placed man, Adam, in the garden paradise, but announced, "It is not good that the man should be alone" (Genesis 2:18). The goodness of man's creation was not fulfilled until God made woman. Male and female are thus created in the image and likeness of God Himself. Man in solitude is incomplete and something less than good. You could say that human nature is designed for community. Human friendship and other bonds can manifest this, but not as fully as the marriage of a man and a woman. Marriage is instituted to provide mutual companionship, help, and support to individuals.

2. Delight

> ". . . ordained so that man and woman may find delight in one another. Therefore, all persons who marry shall take a spouse in holiness and honor, not in the passion of lust, for God has not called us to impurity but in holiness."

Men like women. And women like men. That is the way of God's created order. He wants men and women to meet, court, fall in love, marry, have children, and serve each other until death parts them. Christianity affirms romantic love and its important place in marriage.

Some of King Solomon's most beautiful poetry rejoices in the love between a man and a woman (cf. Song of Solomon 4:1–7). Christian theologians usually interpret the Song of Solomon as God's expression of love to His Bride, the Church, which only makes the sensual tone of it more surprising. Marriage is given as a holy estate wherein a man and a woman can please and enjoy each other.

3. Having Children

> ". . . for the procreation of children who are to be brought up in the fear and instruction of the Lord so that they may offer Him their praise."

God, out of love, created all things. Love is not stagnant. It is the nature of love to grow and spread and bear fruit. God continues to create life and preserve that which He has made.

Men and women are privileged to play a role in God's ongoing creative work, bringing new life out of the flesh, bone, and blood of mothers and fathers. God's love for the world is evidenced by the blossoming of life in our world. Children, by their very existence, declare the presence of a wonderful Creator Lord who loves life.

In addition to the immeasurable joy, it is also a tremendous responsibility to participate in God's continuous project of generating new life. Children are the result of God's divine plan and expressions of His kindness. He expects mothers and fathers to raise these little ones in the knowledge of their true heavenly Father, to know the ways and will of their Creator, and to lead productive lives of thankfulness and charity. "Train up a child in the way he should go; even when he is old he will not depart from it" (Proverbs 22:6).

4. Proclaiming the Gospel

> " . . . a picture of the communion between Christ and His bride, the Church."

This is actually the first purpose of marriage mentioned in the pastor's opening address, but it is included here last for emphasis. Beginning with the rite of Holy Matrimony celebrated in the public worship service and continuing through your whole life together, your very union presents an image to everyone that God, in Christ, has chosen the Church to be His beautiful bride. In Ephesians 5:22–33, St. Paul considers the mysterious similarity of human marriage and Christ's relationship with the Church. Read this passage carefully, for it is one of the texts recommended for the wedding service.

If this wedding rite is being used as an independent service (or when the rite precedes a regularly scheduled service of the congregation), the following or other appropriate passages from Holy Scripture are now read. Each reading may conclude with the response:

L This is the Word of the Lord.
C Thanks be to God.

When the rite stands alone, a sermon is also preached. A hymn may precede or follow. The wedding party may be seated throughout.

Readings from Holy Scripture and the Sermon

Recommended texts:

Genesis 2:7, 18–24; or 1:26–28

1 Corinthians 13

Ephesians 5:1–2, 21–33

Matthew 19:4–6

Mark 10:1–9

John 2

The three traditional Scripture readings appointed for the service of Holy Matrimony reflect a Lutheran arrangement of texts with the emphasis on commandment, cross, and consolation. In the first reading, Genesis 2:7, 18–24, God creates and establishes "the one flesh union" of a husband and a wife as the foundation for all human community. Marriage, then, stabilizes and protects this relationship because God Himself establishes it as His natural order. This is clearly seen in God's Sixth Commandment where all sexual activity—whether of the heart, of the mind, or of the body—is reserved exclusively for a husband and wife within the bonds of their marriage.

The second traditional reading is Matthew 19:4–6. In this reading, Jesus' affirmation of marriage in the face of divorce acknowledges the impact of sin upon marriage. Sin leads us to rebel against God's order. This is the cross that all those who are married must bear. This rebellion leads to all the suffering and hardships that put a strain on the "one flesh union" that is marriage, perverts it, and would not value the good gifts that God intends for those who are married. "What therefore God has joined together, let not man separate" (Matthew 19:6).

In Ephesians 5:1–2, 21–33, both wives and husbands hear the good news that they are not left alone with the devil to do battle and strive to keep God's commandment. But in Jesus Christ, who through His death and resurrection has joined all believers to Himself, a husband and a wife have a model for marriage: Christ and the Church. It is then also in faith that He who blesses marriage and makes it holy will also defend us from the evil one. Our consolation in marriage is the same consolation we have as children of God: that our whole life, even our suffering, can be used by Him to strengthen faith and serve one another.

Hymns

Many weddings today are merely spectacles for the guests to observe. Singing hymns may seem peculiar, but it is always fitting to sing as a congregation when gathered in the triune name and for the purpose of hearing God's Word, even when that occasion is also used for blessing a couple in marriage. Consideration should be given to the singing abilities of those present, the number of guests, or if a large percentage of those in attendance are not members of the congregation. Wherever possible, it is beneficial to include those who are gathered in the church's collective proclamation and praise of hymn singing.

The pastor asks the bridegroom:

P _Name of bridegroom_, will you have this woman to be your wedded wife, to live together in the holy estate of matrimony as God ordained it? Will you nourish and cherish her as Christ loved His body, the Church, giving Himself up for her? Will you love, honor, and keep her in sickness and in health and, forsaking all others, remain united to her alone, so long as you both shall live? Then say: I will.

R *I will.* [Ephesians 5:29]

The pastor asks the bride:

P _Name of bride_, will you have this man to be your wedded husband, to live together in the holy estate of matrimony as God ordained it? Will you submit to him as the Church submits to Christ? Will you love, honor, and keep him in sickness and in health and, forsaking all others, remain united to him alone, so long as you both shall live? Then say: I will.

R *I will.* [Ephesians 5:24]

COMMITMENT: PROMISES AND VOWS

A person is only as good as his or her word. When someone gives you his word, you expect that to be reliable—that is, after all, the pledge of faithfulness. In all of human discourse, there are few things more reprehensible than a liar. "But as for the cowardly, the faithless, the detestable, as for murderers, the sexually immoral, sorcerers, idolaters, and all liars, their portion will be in the lake that burns with fire and sulfur, which is the second death" (Revelation 21:7–9).

In the wedding service, promises are publicly made. The bride and groom are asked nearly identical questions.

The pastor may address the parents of the bridegroom and bride as follows:

P Do you give your consent and blessing to this couple? Then say: We do.

R *We do.*

P Will you pray for and encourage _name_ and _name_ in their marriage, remembering at all times that God wills them to live within their vows until they are parted by death? Then say: We will.

R *We will.*

After the couple has publicly stated their willing and deliberate desire to live in mutual love, the parents of the bridegroom and bride may be invited to add their public consent and promise to the marriage.

The pastor leads the bridegroom and bride to the altar. The bridegroom, taking the right hand of the bride and facing her, says after the pastor:

I, ___*name of bridegroom*___,
take you, ___*name of bride*___,
to be my wedded wife,
to have and to hold from this day forward,
for better, for worse,
for richer, for poorer,
in sickness and in health,
to love and to cherish,
till death us do part,
according to God's holy will;
and I pledge to you my faithfulness.

The bride, in the same way, says after the pastor:

I, ___*name of bride*___,
take you, ___*name of bridegroom*___,
to be my wedded husband,
to have and to hold from this day forward,
for better, for worse,
for richer, for poorer,
in sickness and in health,
to love and to cherish,
till death us do part,
according to God's holy will;
and I pledge to you my faithfulness.

After the parents have spoken their consent, then the traditional vows follow.

In John 8, Jesus calls the devil the father of lies. Satan is a deceiver. Any person who does not keep his word is comparable to Satan and will face wrath. Such strong language is indeed necessary because of how lightly so many people take these noble words spoken on the day of their wedding. When you stand before God and your invited witnesses, you are making a promise to be faithful to this one person until death, no matter what. Carefully consider what that means.

The rings are presented to the pastor; then the following prayer is said:

P Almighty Father, You have generously created all things to serve us for our good. Send Your blessing upon this couple who shall wear these ☩ rings as a constant reminder of their marital fidelity. Grant that by Your mercy they may live gladly and faithfully in this holy estate; through Jesus Christ, Your Son, our Lord, who lives and reigns with You and the Holy Spirit, one God, now and forever. (525)

C **Amen.**

The bridegroom and bride exchange rings beginning with the bridegroom. While giving the ring, each says after the pastor one of the following:

Receive this ring
as a pledge and token
of wedded love and faithfulness.
In the name of the Father
and of the Son
and of the Holy Spirit. Amen.

With this ring I marry you,
my worldly goods I give to you,
and with my body I honor you.
In the name of the Father
and of the Son
and of the Holy Spirit. Amen.

The couple kneels.

EXCHANGE OF RINGS

The rite in *Lutheran Service Book* includes this prayer at the time for exchanging the rings. In it the pastor asks God's blessing, once more, upon you and upon your mutual life together as Christian husband and wife.

The Scriptures do not require the use of wedding rings. This practice is a human custom that spans many centuries and crosses cultures. Typically, people will indicate that the rings, as circles, signify eternity. As a symbol of spousal commitment, we support that sentiment. Human marriage is not literally eternal, however. Only God is without beginning and without end. And God's Word teaches that human marriage does not continue beyond this life. However, the rings could remind us of the unending commitment Christ has made to His Church to forever love her and provide for her. But these pieties are not especially crucial when it comes to the rings themselves. It is sufficient that they are strongly embedded in our culture and psyche as symbols of the commitment between a man and a woman in matrimony.

P Now that _name_ and _name_ have committed themselves to each other in holy matrimony, have given themselves to each other by their solemn pledges, and have declared the same before God and these witnesses, I pronounce them to be husband and wife, in the name of the Father and of the ☩ Son and of the Holy Spirit.

C **Amen.**

P What God has joined together, let no one put asunder. *Matthew 19:6*

C **Amen.**

Announcement

The pastor acts, in part, in the place of the state, because marriage is a temporal estate. His pronouncement is not a magical act. What makes you married is not the words of the minister or anything the pastor has done. What makes you married is your pledge to each other and the public recognition of that pledge. The pastor's role and that of the Church is to proclaim the Gospel, speak God's blessing upon you, celebrate the gift of marriage that our heavenly Father has established for our benefit, and be the principle witnesses of your pledges of fidelity to each other.

Note also that the pastor immediately quotes the words of Jesus about the lifetime commitment of marriage. At the same time, he reminds us that God is, in fact, the one at work in joining the couple into one flesh. Although it is a temporal estate, it is still holy. For God regularly uses the agencies of this world to work His blessings for His creation.

The pastor blesses the couple.

P The almighty and gracious God abundantly grant you His favor and sanctify and bless you with the blessing given to Adam and Eve in Paradise, that you may please Him in both body and soul and live together in holy love until your life's end.

C **Amen.**

P The Lord bless you and keep you.
The Lord make His face shine upon you and be gracious unto you.
The Lord lift up His countenance upon you and ☩ give you peace.

C **Amen.** *Numbers 6:24–26*

BLESSINGS

At the end of the wedding service, the pastor speaks words of blessing to the couple one final time. Reminding us of the creation account by mentioning our first parents, the pastor reminds us also of God's purposes for marriage.

Fittingly, the pastor pronounces this general benediction upon the whole assembly. We finish as we began, in the blessed name of the Holy Trinity, from whom all good things come and into whom the faithful have been baptized.

WHAT ABOUT THE KISS?

Local congregational customs may vary, but this writer finds nothing objectionable in this tradition as long as the bounds of good taste are observed. It conveys the message of Scripture frankly: "As the bridegroom rejoices over the bride, so shall your God rejoice over you" (Isaiah 62:5b). The kiss should occur only after the Benediction is spoken and when the pastor introduces the new couple to the congregation.

Roles and Responsibilities

Misplaced expectations can create tremendous tension in a relationship. When it comes to the roles of husband and wife, most people use their own parents as the standard. We generally assume the roles in the household will resemble those in the home in which we were raised. But obviously, your beloved's family may have done things very differently than yours. It is extremely helpful to think about these things prior to the wedding.

For instance, which of you is going to be responsible for the cooking, the laundry, and the cleaning? Whose job is it to take out the trash, mow the lawn, and balance the checkbook? Running a household is a lot of work. It requires an equitable division of labor. It does not matter so much how the roles are defined as that the definitions are mutually agreeable.

Men and Women Are Unique

Contemporary views about men and women tend to blur all distinctions, to define equality as sameness. Traditionally, people have understood that men and women are unique, that their differences are what make life interesting, that we do think, feel, and experience life in our own respective ways. A man and a woman complement each other. It is not a competition. It is not about superiority and inferiority. It is about celebrating our differences and embracing those ways in which we help and strengthen each other. In the garden, when the Creator states it is not good for the man to be alone, He does not create another man.

He makes the woman from the man. She is delightfully different and yet the man's true partner. Twelfth-century theologian Peter Lombard gave his opinion on why God made Eve from Adam's rib instead of some other part of his body. He believed that God did not take the woman from the man's head, lest she rule over him. God did not take the woman from the man's foot, lest he walk on her. But the Lord God, in His goodness and wisdom, took Eve from Adam's side to indicate that she is his companion.[1]

Do men and women "complete" each other, like missing pieces to a puzzle? The answer is yes and no. As individuals, we find our fullness in God. Take a moment and consider closely Colossians 2:9–10 below, taken from four different and highly reputable Bible translations. How do people receive fullness or completion according to St. Paul?

For in Him the whole fullness of deity dwells bodily, **and you have been filled in Him**, who is the head of all rule and authority. (ESV)

For in Christ all the fullness of the Deity lives in bodily form, **and you have been given fullness in Christ**, who is the head over every power and authority. (NIV)

For in Him all the fullness of Deity dwells in bodily form, **and in Him you have been made complete**, and He is the head over all rule and authority. (NASB)

For in Him dwells all the fullness of the Godhead bodily; **and you are complete in Him**, who is the head of all principality and power. (NKJV™)

These different versions all emphasize the same thought: we are complete, filled, given fullness in Christ.

1 Peter Lombard, cf. *Sentences,* Second Book, Section 18, Chapter 2.

People idolize independence, but is anyone truly independent? Even the natural world shows that everything exists in a delicate balance. An event in one part of the globe—say, a volcanic eruption—affects the lives of many creatures, large and small, in faraway corners and for many years to come. Human interaction is similar. We are constantly affected by others and having an effect on others, whether we are aware of it or not. No man is an island. From the very earliest moment of life, even in the womb, we are dependent on others for nourishment, warmth, shelter, protection, and love. And then we depend on mother and father throughout childhood and beyond. Most of childhood and adolescence is spent learning how to become independent from our parents and to survive on our own, but as emotional beings, we are built for community. The foundation for all human community is the family, and the family is a reflection of the very character of the triune God, the three indivisible persons in eternal community of love, whom we worship and adore.

Some people are quite content to live a single life, but the majority of us sense that something is missing. St. Augustine recognized that every human longing is ultimately a longing for God Himself. He prayed, "Our hearts are restless, O Lord, until they rest in You."[2] He is voicing the sentiment of Psalm 42:1: "As a deer pants for flowing streams, so pants my soul for You, O God." Of course, many people misinterpret their internal longings and attempt to fill the vacancy with money, pleasure, adrenaline, or mind-altering substances. These things appear to offer moments of relief, brief episodes of well-being, but they do not endure, and the feelings of emptiness that follow are greater than before.

Ultimately, worldly pleasures and acquisitions do not give lasting contentment. That peace, *shalom*, that wholeness, comes only as we are incorporated into the Body of Christ. We are baptized into Christ, and now we have oneness and fullness from Him. That is the spring of joy that never goes dry.

Even after emphasizing the sufficiency and necessity of Christ to attain a fulfilling life, human beings are created to dwell in close communion, to find fellowship with one another. The intimate bond that exists between a man and a woman in marriage is especially blessed and rewarding to the heart because of its close resemblance to the self-giving nature of God in Christ to His Bride,

---

2 St. Augustine, *Confessions.*

the Holy Church. Together, male and female, they are called God's image and likeness (Genesis 1:27).

Headship and Authority

Having established how a man and a woman complement each other, the questions again arise: In what sense is the man the head of the family? Isn't that just the cultural residue of ancient barbaric patriarchy?

Although we might find it uncomfortable, the Bible does indeed use headship terminology:

> Wives, submit to your own husbands, as to the Lord. For **the husband is the head of the wife** even as Christ is the head of the church, His body, and is Himself its Savior. Now as the church submits to Christ, so also wives should submit in everything to their husbands. (Ephesians 5:22–24)

Submission, in this sense, does not give the man license to tyrannize his wife. Willing submission is an act of love and respect. Immediately before the verses about husband and wife, Scripture directs all believers to exemplify a spirit of submissiveness out of reverence to Christ (Ephesians 5:21). Submit to one another, the apostle writes. In a marriage, God has put in place a certain order in which the wife heeds her husband's leadership. And he is given the charge to love his wife as Christ loves the Church and gave Himself up for her. This does not mean that wives must do whatever their husbands command. No loving husband would ever want that. Everyone makes sacrifices in a marriage. The husband is called, like Christ, to sacrifice his comforts, wants, and preferences for the benefit of his dear bride. He should put her interests ahead of his own. His greatest desire shall be to serve her and to give her everything he has. In response, the wife listens and follows his example by likewise giving up herself to him. Neither can insist on having his or her own way. Neither can abuse or mistreat the other. Mutual respect and kindness will always characterize their relationship. But the Word of God teaches that the husband is modeled after

Christ's offering of Himself upon the cross. And the wife is modeled after the bride who receives the benefits of the bridegroom's gifts and devotes herself to service and thanksgiving.

Saying that the man is the head of the woman is not about governance. It is about service. This biblical role differentiation is not the basis for assertions of power, but it is a description of avenues for service. The man's God-given avenue for serving his wife is to sacrifice himself for her. And the woman's God-given avenue for serving her husband is yielding to him and receiving the fruit of his sacrificial love. She supports his role as leader of the household. In this way, the welfare of all is served.

Children

Although you may be focused at this point only on your wedding plans, now is precisely the right time to talk about children. Disagreements about having and raising children are among the chief sources of strife in a marriage. Find consensus today and you will avoid potential marital conflict tomorrow.

The term *reproduction* suggests that human beings are commodities that are produced, such as toasters on an assembly line. The term *procreation* is preferable because it indicates the mysterious partnership between human beings and God in this creative act from which new life emerges. Although it may seem old-fashioned in our age of birth control, procreation is a fundamental purpose of marriage. At creation, God spoke to our first parents, "Be fruitful and multiply" (Genesis 1:28). This is more than simply a primordial commandment. It is also a promise. God's Word truly does what it says. Just as God spoke the universe into existence, He is even now, by the power of His spoken Word, causing every living thing in nature to grow and multiply.

Love is not love until it is given away. One could suggest that the purpose for which God created the world was to pour out His love on humanity. That is the natural course for love. And when a man and a woman, fashioned in God's likeness, come together in love and become one flesh, they generate a new life, someone other than themselves, to whom they devote themselves in service.

God blesses couples with children. "Behold, children are a heritage from the Lord, the fruit of the womb a reward" (Psalm 127:3). Oh, how different are the ways and thoughts of God from ours. A culture of death has encompassed much of Western society. Pregnancy is often considered an inconvenience. Children limit personal freedom and deplete the bank account. Selfish disdain for children has led to a troubling decrease in births in western Europe, Russia, Japan, and, to a lesser extent, North America. A low birthrate will harm these societies as their population ages and there is less money contributed to pension funds, both public and private. But having children is good—for society and for the Church. It is good for you. It pleases the Lord to see our families grow.

Children are a blessing from God, not a burden or nuisance. Christians differ on the appropriateness of birth control within marriage, but family planning is wise. Before you marry, give serious discussion to when and how many children you hope to have.

The Bible teaches us to exercise humility when planning our lives:

> Come now, you who say, "Today or tomorrow we will go into such and such a town and spend a year there and trade and make a profit"—yet you do not know what tomorrow will bring. What is your life? For you are a mist that appears for a little time and then vanishes. Instead you ought to say, "If the Lord wills, we will live and do this or that." As it is, you boast in your arrogance. All such boasting is evil. (James 4:13–16)

God is not pleased when we attempt to act as lord of our lives. He is pleased when people trust Him with their future. Only God knows what tomorrow brings. And we are confident that God is immeasurably good. Thus His plans for us are good, even when they might be uncomfortable for us at the time.

The point is that even the most attentive and careful family planning is fallible. Yet pregnancy is a blessing from God and must never be despised, even when its timing is not of our choosing. Abortion to terminate an unplanned pregnancy is never a moral option. Since every human life is precious in the eyes of the Creator, rejecting a child is tantamount to rejecting God. Abortion is vile murder and must be viewed as such. God abhors it, and so must we.

CONCLUSION

Contending with sin and the temptations of the world is daunting. Single or engaged, married or widowed, we are in a daily fight against Satan. As a couple, you will be in that battle too. You might not face addiction or gross infidelity, but perhaps you will confront workaholism or selfishness. Does this mean you should not get married? No, but it does mean you should approach your marriage thoughtfully and prayerfully. The purpose of this book is to help you spot the weak areas in your relationship so that you can grow and improve before making the commitment of marriage. People naively say that all that matters is that they love each other. Love is crucial, of course, but love often requires us to work out tough questions with brutal honesty. With Christ, that which appears daunting is possible.

Take time together to discuss openly and honestly each of the topics raised in this book. How might certain temptations or weaknesses be present in your lives? What can you do to prevent them from exercising control over you? Identify the strengths God has given to each of you and how these contribute to the strength of your relationship. Get into the habit early in your relationship of praying together. Ask God to give you wisdom and courage to live purely, to live according to His will, to help you love each other selflessly, to achieve balance, to turn away from those things that are destructive. Call upon God as your source of daily strength to overcome the obstacles you face. Thank Him for the wonderful gifts He has given to each of you individually and as a couple. Pray with and for each other daily, and you will make gigantic strides past many potential marriage pitfalls.

PRAYERS FOR ENGAGED COUPLES

GENERAL

Almighty and most gracious Father, You gave our first parents, Adam and Eve, to each other for the purposes of companionship and love. We thank You for bringing us together and for the love that we share. Continue to bless us always with Your presence, and may our lives together bring honor to Your name. Guide us as we plan for our wedding day. Keep safe those guests who will travel to celebrate our happiness with us. We make these requests in the name of Your Son, our Lord Jesus Christ, who lives and reigns with You and the Holy Spirit, one God, now and forever. Amen.

FOR PATIENCE

Dear Lord in heaven, You are so patient with us when we stumble and fail. You never cease demonstrating Your loving-kindness by the ways You daily provide for our needs of body and spirit. In like manner, help us to be patient with each other, with circumstances beyond our control, and with the weaknesses and idiosyncrasies of the people around us. Give us humble hearts, like the heart of our dear Savior. Make us slow to anger and quick to forgive. Help us pay more attention to the logs in our own eyes than the specks in the eyes of others. As we have been forgiven, according to Your mercy, help us to forgive those who offend us. In the name of Jesus Christ, Your Son, our Lord, who lives and reigns with You and the Holy Spirit, one God, now and forever. Amen.

FOR HARMONY

Our dear Father, it pleases You when Your children live in unity and peace. Give us the Spirit of peace when we become upset or troubled. Dispel all useless worry from our beings. We know that panic and fear are tools the devil uses to fracture our families and alienate us from You. So be our source of harmony when the devil and the cares of this world would otherwise upset us. Thank You for the sacrifice upon the cross of Your Son, whose blood reconciles us to You forever. May that reconciliation become the basis for ours to be a strong and harmonious family, that You alone may be glorified. In the name of Jesus Christ, Your Son, our Lord, who lives and reigns with You and the Holy Spirit, one God, now and forever. Amen.

For Faith

Strengthen us in true faith, dearest Lord. Hold us close to the pure doctrine and practice of Your Holy Word. Defend us from the deceiver, Satan, who tries to pull us away from You. Shield us from the temptations and the enticements of the world that would injure our relationship with You. May we, by Your grace alone, stand firm in our convictions based on Scripture. Send Your Holy Spirit to reinforce our trust in Your kindness so that we may never stray. When we falter, may we always look to You for redemption. In the name of Jesus Christ, Your Son, our Lord, who lives and reigns with You and the Holy Spirit, one God, now and forever. Amen.

For the Future

Only You, loving Master, know all things. Only You can foresee all outcomes. There are many things about the future that make us anxious or afraid. It is the fear of the unknown. But we believe that nothing is unknown to You. This comforts us because we know that You love us as a Father loves His children, and You will guide us tenderly along the paths of Your choosing. We acknowledge our dependence upon You. Assure us that You love us and that nothing can pluck us from Your tender care. Our attempts to grasp control so often result in disaster. But You are the calm in every storm. Increase our faith. In the name of Jesus Christ, Your Son, our Lord, who lives and reigns with You and the Holy Spirit, one God, now and forever. Amen.

When Anxious

Father in heaven, You promise to hear us when we pray. You demonstrated Your power when Your Son calmed the storm that frightened the disciples on the Sea of Galilee. Please bring calm and peace to our hearts and to those dear to us. The stresses of life are heavy. We cast our cares upon You. Remind us of Your abiding presence, Your unfailing strength, and Your desire to bless us as our dear heavenly Father. In the name of Jesus Christ, Your Son, our Lord, who lives and reigns with You and the Holy Spirit, one God, now and forever. Amen.

For Our Extended Families

Dear devoted Father, You established the family to care for the young and to illustrate Your love for all humanity. Thank You for our parents and grandparents, our aunts and uncles, our siblings, cousins, and future in-laws. Through them, You have brought us to this point in our lives. Help us to forgive the injuries of the past, the imperfections that plague every home, and to accept our responsibility for our own flaws and errors. May our union in holy marriage bring honor and joy to our parents and guardians. In the name of Jesus Christ, Your Son, our Lord, who lives and reigns with You and the Holy Spirit, one God, now and forever. Amen.

For Our Wedding Party

Gracious King, thank You for friendship. Thank You for the special friends You have given to us, people who care about us and wish us happiness. You know their individual needs and personal hardships. Help them. Look favorably upon them so that they may always find true fulfillment in knowing You, through the merits of Your Son, through whom we pray. Amen.

Giving Thanks

Dear merciful Creator, we know that every good and perfect gift comes from You. You generously provide all that we need to sustain this body and life. Most especially, we thank You for having called us out of darkness into Your marvelous light, for redeeming us from death and condemnation through the atoning sacrifice of Your Son upon the cross. Thank You for the Means of Grace, the Gospel as it comes to us through Baptism, preaching, Absolution, and Communion. Apart from You, we can do nothing, but You have made us Your children and promise us forgiveness, life, and everlasting glory. As a couple, we are particularly grateful also for the love that we share and our life together. Please smile upon us and be gracious to us so that all that we do may bring glory to Your holy name. Through Jesus Christ, Your Son, our Lord, who lives and reigns with You and the Holy Spirit, now and forever. Amen.

WEDDING QUESTIONS AND ANSWERS

✣ Who Is the Focus of the Service?

For Christians, Jesus Christ is the focal point in every Christian service, including weddings. This Christ-centeredness will influence every aspect of the wedding, just as it does every liturgical gathering. At the joyous occasion of the joining of a man and a woman in holy matrimony, God's mercy in Christ, the Bridegroom, and the repentant faith of the Church, Christ's Bride, is always in mind.

✣ Where Should the Wedding Take Place?

A legally performed ceremony is valid whether it takes place in the chancel or at a local campground. Your pastor is the best person to explain the local situation. It is important to respect the guidelines and sensitivities of your pastor and the congregation.

An outdoor wedding might seem fun and romantic, but the logistics may be more complicated than having the ceremony in the church. You will want to consider unpredictable weather conditions, insects, and even wind. The acoustics are likely to be poor, the seating uncomfortable, and so on. You will probably discover that it is more practical to have your wedding in the place where God's Word is weekly proclaimed. Being surrounded by the sacred art and furnishings will help maintain the Christ-centeredness of the service.

✤ When Is It Appropriate to Have the Wedding?

While there are no definite rules about when to schedule a wedding, there are some things to keep in mind as you save the date for the big day. Consider the Church Year. The season of Lent is the time when we place special emphasis on the sufferings of our Lord Jesus in preparation for Good Friday and Easter. Lent is a penitential season in the Church. Holy Week, the days just before Easter, is particularly somber. Given the exceedingly joyous character of marriage, many congregations will not choose to schedule a wedding during Lent and Holy Week.

✤ Can We Invite a Pastor of Another Denomination to Participate?

Sadly, the Christian Church has suffered many divisions over the centuries. Such is the state of sinful humanity. It is God-pleasing to desire peace and to work toward greater unity, but we must never do so at the expense of the truth. Outward institutional unity that overlooks serious differences of teaching and belief does not achieve true unity. St. Paul wrote: "I appeal to you, brothers, by the name of our Lord Jesus Christ, that all of you agree, and that there be no divisions among you, but that you be united in the same mind and the same judgment" (1 Corinthians 1:10). Unity of the spirit is founded on a mutual agreement on what God says. It would give a false impression of unity, therefore, for Christian pastors of different denominations to co-officiate at a wedding. If you have someone in mind, perhaps a relative or friend of the family, rather than asking him to assist in the ceremony, you could ask him to give a toast at the reception.

✤ What Is Appropriate Decorum in Church?

Christians behave reverently in God's house. The building itself, whether plain or ornate, is sanctified (that is, set aside and made holy) by virtue of God's Word and the prayers of God's people. In all that you do, show proper respect for the place where the Gospel is declared, the washing of regeneration occurs, and where the body and blood of Christ are made present for the saints to eat and drink. Solemnity does not mean joylessness, but it does mean showing honor for the things of God.

✤ What about the Wedding Party's Attire?

Styles and fashions vary across time and place. The attire of the wedding party may be more or less formal. Keep in mind that not everything that is fashionable is in good taste.

Many women understandably have sentimental attachment to their wedding dress. Universally, brides adorn themselves radiantly for their husbands. It is a fitting image of the righteousness with which God clothes the Church in preparation for the great wedding banquet in heaven. "And I saw the holy city, new Jerusalem, coming down out of heaven from God, prepared as a bride adorned for her husband" (Revelation 21:2).

✤ What about Cameras during the Service?

It is distracting to snap photos excessively during the service itself. Flash photography especially should be discouraged between the Invocation at the beginning of the service and the Benediction at the end. Local customs may vary, but the families and guests should respect the restrictions of the congregation and pastor. There is always ample time for photographs before and after the service proper. Frequently, there is no objection to an unobtrusive video camera on a tripod in the balcony or the transept. But the pastor should approve all photography and filming arrangements.

✤ Which Music Can Be Used?

No music should be selected or planned without first consulting the pastor. As God's called minister in that place, it is the pastor's responsibility to oversee all public services of the congregation. The pastor may wish to include the church's musician in the selection process.

The fundamental principle to remember is that Jesus Christ is the center of every gathering in God's house. As tempting as it may be, the primary focus is not on the bride and groom. Many contemporary weddings incorporate secular love songs into the service. However, all solos or special music in a church wedding should maintain the Christ-centered focus. Always ask the question: how does this song declare the Gospel—the good news that Jesus came to save sinners? There is plenty of opportunity for enjoying popular love songs at the rehearsal dinner, the wedding reception, and so on.

✤ How Shall the Processional Be Done?

The pastor will be able to direct the wedding party as to the particulars in the rehearsal. The specific layout of the building may require unique instructions. In general, it is good for groomsmen to escort the bridesmaids in a procession following a processional crucifix (or cross), if one is available. The congregation rises at the entrance of the cross. The groom may arrive at the chancel from the side or enter as part of the processional, following the attendants. Traditionally, the bride is escorted by her father, who then "gives her away" to the groom as they reach the chancel. The men line up at the pastor's left hand as he faces the congregation and the women at the pastor's right. If the wedding rite occurs within a longer service (Matins, Vespers, etc.), the wedding party may sit in the front of the nave in reserved pews or in special seating provided for them.

✣ Should We Have the Lord's Supper at Our Wedding?

There are sound reasons why celebrating a Christian wedding in the context of a Divine Service makes sense. The Sacrament of the Altar is a foretaste of the feast to come. We look forward to that great and glorious day when our Lord, the Bridegroom, comes to take His Bride, the Church, and celebrate what the Scriptures call the wedding feast of the Lamb. That is our greatest hope as followers of Jesus Christ. That celebratory meal of fellowship, enjoyed by the saints in heaven, is what the Church on earth participates in even now at the Lord's table. Because your wedding is a mirror image of the mystic union of Christ and the Church, celebrating the rite of Holy Matrimony in a service that also celebrates the Lord's Supper seems natural.

The difficulty is that wedding guests often come from a diversity of religious beliefs and practices. It is scriptural for only those in doctrinal agreement to commune together. Guests who would, with good intentions, come to the altar might be in danger of consuming the Lord's body and blood in a way that would be harmful to them. The kindest act is to ensure that all who come to the table are properly instructed in the Gospel and the meaning of the Sacrament beforehand. Unless you are confident that those guests you have invited for your special day will be eligible to commune with the congregation, it seems impractical to have your marriage service within the Divine Service.

✣ When Do We Present the Wedding License?

Most pastors will expect to receive the wedding license at, or by the time of, the rehearsal. It is not legal to conduct the service without a license from the state.

PLANNING THE WEDDING

ANNOUNCEMENT

Most likely, you will first want to share the news of your engagement with your parents and close friends. High on the list of those to whom you announce your engagement should also be your pastor. Confirm as quickly as possible his availability and the church's for your proposed wedding date.

There is a tradition of announcing marriage banns in the church where the wedding will take place. The word *banns* comes from an Old English word meaning "to summon." Marriage banns refer to the public notification in a congregation that two specified individuals plan to marry on a certain date, usually three weeks in advance. This is intended to give the community an opportunity to present any legal impediment. Examples of such impediments would be that one or the other is already married, the lack of consent, or that their blood relationship falls within the prohibited degree of kinship. The *Lutheran Service Book: Agenda* recommends the following wording:

P On *date*, *legal name of the man* and *legal name of the woman* desire to enter the holy estate of matrimony according to the Lord's Word. They desire our prayers so that they may begin their marriage in God's name and with His blessing. If you can show just cause why these two persons should not be joined together in holy matrimony, you are to declare it before the wedding. May God grant them His blessing.

P Let us pray.

Heavenly Father, You established matrimony and desire that we keep it holy. Behold with Your favor *name* and *name*, who intend to have their union blessed by Your Word. Grant them Your grace so that they may begin their wedded life in You, live according to Your Word, and rejoice in Your strong love and enduring blessing; through Jesus Christ, Your Son, our Lord, who lives and reigns with You and the Holy Spirit, one God, now and forever. (524)

C **Amen.**

Wedding Information

This marriage information form is designed to be used by those who are planning a wedding in the church and gives valuable information to the pastor and those who assist him in this task. While all the information may not be available immediately, it is often best to provide even a little information early on.

GROOM

Full name: ______________________

Phone: ______________________

E-mail: ______________________

Street address: ______________________

City/State/Zip: ______________________

Date of birth: ______________________

Place of birth: ______________________

Religion/Denomination: ______________________

Church: ______________________

Occupation: ______________________

Place of employment: ______________________

Work phone: ______________________

Father's name: ______________________

Mother's first and maiden name: ______________________

Have you ever been engaged to be married before?

☐ Yes ☐ No How long? ______________________

Reason for termination? ______________________

Have you ever been married before?

☐ Yes ☐ No How long? ______________________

Reason for termination? ______________________

Additional notes: ______________________

BRIDE

Full name: ______________________

Phone: ______________________

E-mail: ______________________

Street address: ______________________

City/State/Zip: ______________________

Date of birth: ______________________

Place of birth: ______________________

Religion/Denomination: ______________________

Church: ______________________

Occupation: ______________________

Place of employment: ______________________

Work phone: ______________________

Father's name: ______________________

Mother's first and maiden name: ______________________

Have you ever been engaged to be married before?

☐ Yes ☐ No How long? ______________________

Reason for termination? ______________________

Have you ever been married before?

☐ Yes ☐ No How long? ______________________

Reason for termination? ______________________

Additional notes: ______________________

Wedding Information

How long have you known each other? ______

New address of married couple: ______

City/State/Zip: ______

Phone: ______

Marriage Service

First reading: ______

Second reading: ______

Third reading: ______

Congregational hymns: ______

______

______

Soloist/Choir: ______

Is the bride being "given away"? ☐ Yes ☐ No If yes, by whom? ______

Will parents voice their consent in the service? ☐ Yes ☐ No

Ring ceremony: ☐ Single ☐ Double

Unity candle: ☐ Yes ☐ No

Other: ______

______

______

______

Is the bride wearing a veil? ☐ Yes ☐ No

Are the bride and groom able to kneel? ☐ Yes ☐ No

Is the bride carrying a bouquet? ☐ Yes ☐ No

Wedding bulletins ☐ Yes ☐ No

WEDDING INFORMATION

INFORMATION FOR CONGREGATION'S WEDDING ASSISTANT

Names of couple: ______________________________

Wedding date and time: ______________________________

Rehearsal date and time: ______________________________

Color scheme: ______________________________

Florist: ______________________________

Photographer: ______________________________

Videographer: ______________________________

ATTENDANTS: (Please use given names—not nicknames)

1. Best man: ______________________________

2. Maid or Matron (circle one) of honor: ______________________________

3. Groomsmen (in order):

____

____

____

____

____

____

4. Bridesmaids (in order):

____

____

____

____

____

____

WEDDING INFORMATION

5. Ringbearer: _______________ (age ____)

Flower girl: _______________ (age ____)

6. Ushers (other than groomsmen): _______________

____

____

____

____

7. Aisle runner (____ ft) ☐ Yes ☐ No   If runner, is florist installing? ☐ Yes ☐ No

Who will pin flowers on members of wedding party? _______________

8. Unity candle ☐ Yes ☐ No   Providing own unity candle? ☐ Yes ☐ No

Aisle candle ☐ Yes ☐ No   Wedding candelabra ☐ Yes ☐ No

9. Special seating arrangements (handicapped persons/large number of parents and grandparents/persons especially assigned to escort mothers down aisle): _______________

____

10. Will there be a receiving line at the church? ☐ Yes ☐ No

11. Will the wedding party be dressing at the church? ☐ Yes ☐ No

12. Will pictures be taken before or after the ceremony? ☐ Before ☐ After ☐ No

13. Will there be bulletins for the service? ☐ Yes ☐ No   How many needed? ____   Providing own bulletins? ☐ Yes ☐ No

14. Will a video be made? ☐ Yes ☐ No

15. Will flowers be left at the church? ☐ Yes ☐ No

MUSIC:

1. Has music director been contacted? ☐ Yes ☐ No

2. Soloist: _______________ Contacted? ☐ Yes ☐ No

3. Has a list of music and solos been submitted? ☐ Yes ☐ No

ll hymns be sung during the service? ☐ Yes ☐ No